Let's Talk Behaviour!

LE3022

ISBN: 978-1-903670-93-4

© Wendy Usher

Illustrations © Peter Scott

All rights reserved

First published 2015

Printed in the UK for Lawrence Educational
PO Box 532, Cambridge, CB1 0BX, UK

Acknowledgements

With thanks to Widgit Software for the use of their symbols.

Widgit Symbols © Widgit Software 2002–2015 www.widgit.com

Printed under licence by The Play Doctors Ltd

Permission to photocopy

Contents

Introduction

We all have difficult days and as adults we are normally able to control our temper even if we would like to have a full blown tantrum just to 'let it out'! Children are not defined by the same rules and often show us how they are feeling through their behaviour. Behaviour itself is a form of communication and, if this is the case, we need to know what the communication is behind the behaviour.

In this book I draw on over 30 years of experience in working with children to share some ideas and suggestions to consider ways to support effective communication and promote positive behaviour. Some suggestions are activities to do with the children and others are challenges for the reader to consider how their own behaviour and communication may be affecting the children's responses.

Throughout the book I advocate taking a child-centred approach and looking at the situation through the child's eyes. Sometimes behaviour is not a self-willed act of defiance; sometimes it is a cry for help. In taking a child-centred approach, we are able to look at the possible reasons for the behaviour, such as an underlying impairment or sensory overload. The reasons behind the behaviour will vary, sometimes reflecting frustration where the child's life is adult led and there is little in the form of the child making their own choices or having their own control.

Case studies have been used throughout the book to help the reader reflect on the ideas suggested. I have also included 'think' boxes which help you take the ideas further and think about approaching situations from a different angle.

A list of further resources which you may find useful is given at the end of the book.

How Do We Communicate?

Thinking about how our children learn

Think about the children in your setting or at home. How many of them are primarily visual (seeing) or kinaesthetic (doing) learners? Probably the majority as most children prefer to learn by seeing and doing, particularly if the child has English as a second language or has an underlying social communication impairment such as autism.

However, what happens when we are dealing with and teaching them about unacceptable or inappropriate behaviour? We tend to respond to children by talking and giving verbal instruction. Not only that, but we tend to use far too many words. If the child is stressed and we are not careful we can give them an auditory sensory overload. This means the child's listening ability reduces and the child may not process the spoken word or meaning behind the language correctly.

Throughout this book we look at how we can reflect the child's key learning style in the way we respond to children.

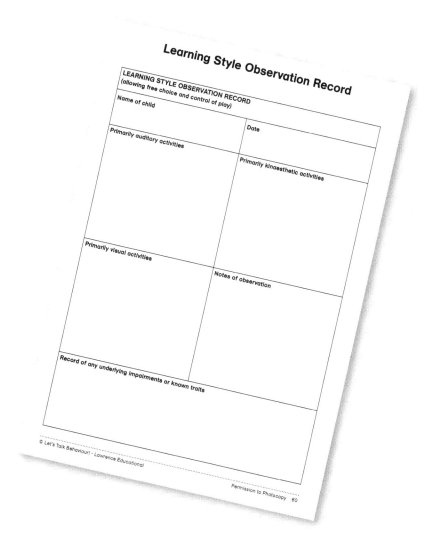

Ideas to Recognise Children's Learning Styles

Resources needed

Learning Style Observation Record (See page 60. Use this template to observe children in free-play activity sessions where the child is free to move around the setting and to choose the activities they wish to participate in.)

Activity and key ideas

We can recognise a child's predominant learning style by watching the way they play. Let's take the simple activity of reading a book. When a child chooses to look at a book observe how they interact with the story:

Visual (seeing)	Visual learners will want to look at the pictures, tell you about them and search for things within the illustrations. They want to talk about the things they see.
Kinaesthetic (doing)	Kinaesthetic learners will want to follow the words with their finger, or hold your finger while you follow the words. They also want to turn the pages. These children may want to illustrate the story for themselves by making animal noises or undertaking actions to accompany the story.
Auditory (hearing)	Auditory learners are happy to listen. They will sit quietly whilst you are reading the story and listen carefully. They are very happy to talk about the story and prefer to have a conversation about it. These children will have taken in more facts and be accurate in their re-telling.

Ask the child to think of a story that they know well. Offer them three simple activities based around the story or main character. This could be:

- painting (visual)
- construction (kinetic)
- listening to the story on a CD (audio).

From the choice offered, see which one the child initially goes to. This will give you a simple understanding of learning-type preferences. In turn this will help you to communicate with the child by focusing on their primary learning style. Please note it is not a failsafe method, but is designed to give you a quick simple overview of the child's preferences.

Using Language – and Keeping it Super Simple

Activity and key ideas

We all know most children like to talk! When they get going it can be hard to stop them. However, are we the same? Do we use twenty words when ten could suffice? We use our voices far too much especially when children are upset or emotional, and particularly if a child is not an auditory learner. The child may not be able to interpret everything you say as their processing ability could be disrupted because of their emotional state.

Remember the acronym **KISS** – Keep It Super Simple. Don't overcomplicate verbal communication, it is not necessary and can overwhelm children so they don't get the key messages.

Start by saying the child's name, keep sentences short, simple and to the point. Don't try to give too many instructions at one time. Try to show children what you want them to do by using actions and expressive body language. Think about what you saying and how you are using words.

Think

Some children may have a social communication difficulty such as autism or may have English as a second language. When stressed or upset these children may not hear the whole sentence and instead only hear and respond to part of it. For example:

Teacher: 'Don't run on the road!'
Nina hears: 'Run on the road!' or 'On the road!'

How could this be rephrased?

Teacher: 'Nina, walk on the pavement!'
Nina hears: 'On the pavement!'

Try to make your communication positive.

Case study

Ben is nearly 5 years old. He has difficultly in listening to too many instructions at one time and tries his best to remember what he has been asked to do. Sometimes, if there are too many he only does the last one or two.

Teacher: 'Ben, please put away your toys, put on your coat, fetch your lunchbox and stand by the door'.

Ben forgets the first three instructions as it was too much to take in. He leaves his toys, forgets his coat and lunchbox and goes to stand by the door. The teacher is frustrated; Ben has not done as she has asked.

Using Noise Makers to Gain Attention

Resources needed

Tambourine, bells, shaker or other noise maker
Tin preferably with a snap-on plastic lid
Buttons, gravel, small stones, rice, pasta or different types of dry beans
Colouring pens and paper
Strong tape or glue
Strong container
Balloon

Activity and key ideas

Our voice is our best tool, however, we tend to misuse it. How often have we tried to get a child's attention by beginning to say their name quietly, and then as they do not respond, raise our voice a little more and a little more until we find ourselves almost shouting! 'Tara, Tara, **Tara!**'

We need to catch and stop ourselves doing this because the child may not understand or know the difference between calling out to gain their attention or asking for immediate compliance such as stopping when they are about to run in the road. In addition, when we shout we are giving the child permission to do the same.

Make a sound maker to use to get attention instead of using your voice.

1. Use an old tin preferably with a snap-on plastic lid. Experiment with different materials inside to shake such as buttons, gravel, small stones, rice, pasta or different types of dry beans. Allow the children to decorate the tins. Seal the lid using tape or glue.

2. Find a strong cylindrical container such as a cardboard gravy granule container or small tin. Cut the neck off a balloon and stretch the body of the balloon across the opening of the container so that it is nice and tight. Tape the edge of the balloon to the container to stop it sliding off. Use the instrument as a drum. Try adding some rice or pasta into the container. It jumps when the drum is hit and adds an extra dimension to the sound.

Be aware when undertaking this activity that some children may be sensitive to certain noises.

Think

Think of the children in your setting who have a lack of self-esteem and confidence. Help them to feel important and make them your 'sound maker' for the session by asking them to shake the instrument when you want to gain attention.

What is the Meaning Behind the Words?

Activity and key ideas

Every child learns differently and has different levels of comprehension and understanding. Some are quicker than others to grasp concepts. Think about the language we sometimes use in managing behaviour: 'Give over!' 'Stop that!' 'You know better.' Now think of those words from a child's perspective. What do they mean? We need to give clear instruction. When dealing with inappropriate behaviour be direct in your communication and make it clear to the child what you want them to do. For example:

Teacher talking to Caleb who has his feet on the table:

Teacher: 'You know better.'
Caleb's thoughts: Why is she talking to me? What does she mean? What am I meant to do?

Or instead:

Teacher: 'Caleb, put your feet on the floor, thank you.' (Provide an instruction, illustrate by your own movement and add a thank you to convey your expectation that Caleb will comply.)

Game – Actions behind the words

Think of range of actions that you would like to see associated with good behaviour such as hands down, feet on floor. Play a game where the child practises the movement associated to words:

Start by saying, 'Show me, show me ...'

Ballerina's hands – demonstrate to the children hands held in front of the body

Soldier's hands – demonstrate a salute followed by hands at sides of body

Soldier's feet. Attention! – demonstrate stamping one foot on ground and standing still with both feet on the ground

Snake charmer – demonstrate sitting cross legged on the floor

If you need a child to comply with a behavioural command such as sit down, you could use the words the child associates with the behaviour – 'Show me, show me a snake charmer!' That way behaviour management is fun. You could also try getting the children to make up their own actions associated to instructions/words.

Let's Make it Clear! Thinking About What We Say

Resources needed

Pre-prepared visual cards either illustrated or photographic

Activity and key ideas

This activity is good for visual learners.

Help the child identify the type of action you wish to see from a visual command. This helps avoid misunderstandings. It is especially useful for children who are literal thinkers or lack imagination, such as those on the autism spectrum or those who have social communication difficulties. For instance, a literal thinker told, 'Go and wash your hands in the toilet' may indeed do just that.

Create a series of visual cards by drawing different actions on paper (or find images on the computer and stick them onto cards). Suggested images include:

- sitting cross legged (sitting nicely)
- a finger placed over the lips (quiet)
- two children shaking hands (friends)
- a number of children standing in a line (lining up nicely)
- a child with their hand behind their ear (listen)
- a child holding their hand up to their eyes (look)
- a child holding their arms horizontally out from their body (space and body awareness)
- a child passing something to another (sharing).

Say to the child, 'Show me, show me ... Quiet.'

The child picks up the appropriate card and makes the associated action. Continue with other words and demonstrate their meaning, 'Show me, show me ... Lining up nicely.'

Once the child has learned the appropriate action via the game, the cards can be used as flash cards to help the child recognise what you are asking them to do.

Self-Evaluation for Communicating Effectively

Resources needed
Communication Assessment Template (see page 61)

Activity and key ideas
This page is dedicated to your own practices, what works well and why, and what does not work quite so well and why.

Think about the children in your care. When communicating with them you use your voice, your facial expressions, gestures and visual clues including objects of reference (such as holding a cup up to indicate drink time).

Use the Communication Assessment Template to think about individual children. When supporting children's behaviour we need to take a child-centred approach and think about what works best.

Take a look at the example right.

COMMUNICATION ASSESSMENT

Name of Child Nathan	Date 20th November
What works well	**What does not work so well**
Getting down to his physical level	Raising your voice (he puts his hands over his ears)
Saying his name first so he knows you are talking to him	Assuming he knows he is included if talking to a group
Giving one instruction at a time	Giving him too many instructions
Reinforcing the instruction by showing him something visual	Using too many words or speaking too fast
Giving him extra time to process information	Expecting an immediate response
Repeating the instruction in the same words if he has not responded	Asking for eye contact. If he looks at you he does not always take in what you are saying

Special ways the child communicates
Sometimes Nathan repeats what you say but it does not mean he has understood it

Listening Skills

Thinking about how our children learn

It is easy to think that we hear through our ears, but the reality is that we 'hear' using everything around us that give us clues.

When we are working with young children it is essential to hear them by listening to them and by *observing* them. We don't always get the correct messages without looking at the whole picture.

> **Behaviour itself is a form of communication – if this is so, what is the communication behind the behaviour?**

Case study

Jenna is 3 years old; she has very little verbal communication and tends to rely on her older sisters to interpret her needs. When she started pre-school the lack of verbal communication became more apparent. She became very frustrated with the lack of adult understanding which was demonstrated in tantrums and screaming fits.

The staff spoke to her mum and collated a list of ways in which Jenna communicates. Examples of non-verbal communication included:

- when Jenna licks the back of her hand she is hungry
- when she constantly licks her lips she is thirsty
- when she sucks on her jumper or T-shirt sleeve she is tired
- when she walks on tippy toes she needs reminding to go to the toilet.

As the staff worked with Jenna, they helped her to vocalise her needs so she became more fluent in her speech. Having the ability to 'listen' to her actions helped staff to interpret her behaviour before she became too frustrated.

Think

If you are aware of any child's specific behaviour that is communicating something – don't keep it to yourself. Share it with other staff in the setting.

Making a Communication Passport

Resources needed

Communication Passport Template (see page 62)
Photo of child

Activity and key ideas

If you happen to know of any particular behaviour that a child exhibits that has a specific meaning, it is important to share with others. Simple communication passports can help to achieve this.

Think

Engage others in this activity. Who knows most about the child? Ask parents and other carers what behaviour they have observed and what the meaning is behind the behaviour.

Make your own communication passports focusing on the important elements for individual children. Take a child-centred approach and change the heading titles to suit a particular child.

All about me

I like to be called
Ru not RuRu or Rutendo just Ru

Things I like doing
Playing with dinosaurs
Drinking from my own yellow beaker

Things I need some help with
Going to the toilet
Feeding myself

This is me!

Name

Things I don't like
Too much noise
Too many people

Things I like
Yellow things
My beaker
Bananas
Yellow lorries

Special ways I communicate
If I am frightened I spin in a circle
If it's too noisy I flap my hands
When I need the toilet I stand still by the door
I don't talk much but I do understand. Please say things clearly and don't give me too many instructions

Special things about me!
I have traits of autism

Things that help calm me down
Holding my dinosaur
Singing action songs

Take a look at the example left and use the photocopy template on page 62 to make your own. Add a picture of the child in the centre and write in their name.

Hearing the Child's Voice 1

Resources needed

2 buckets
Bean bags or balls
Paper and pens
Sticky tape

Activity and key ideas

This fun and playful activity provides an alternative way for children to tell you if they have enjoyed an activity and to help make group decisions and choices.

Draw two large faces onto paper and stick them onto the buckets. The faces should indicate happy and sad. Place the buckets at the end of the room.

Give each of the children a bean bag or ball. When you ask a simple question the children run to place their object into one of the buckets. They choose their own responses.

Suggested questions might include:

- How did you feel when Mrs Usher read the story to you?
- How did you feel when we played with the puppets?
- How would you feel if we had carrots at snack time?

Adapt the activity by changing the signs on the buckets to a tick and cross representing yes and no. Questions can be asked, 'Do you want to ...?'

Think

With older children think about how this activity could be used to discuss social situations and engage the children in conversation. Use character toys or puppets and ask how the toy would feel if ... (giving an example situation). Ask the children to put the characters in one of the buckets.

Take some time to discuss what would need to happen to change the character or puppet from the sad to the happy bucket. Explore different ways of behaving and get the children to make their own decisions and move the characters.

Hearing the Child's Voice 2

Resources needed

A large tree displayed on a wall

Several different leaves each indicating a different activity available to the child

Activity and key ideas

Many young children find it hard to make decisions when faced with too many choices. Coming into a vibrant, busy and noisy setting is not always easy. Children are often surrounded by too much sensory stimuli, and especially when first entering a setting, it can become too much. The child's 'voice' is often heard in the form of hiding behind mum, hands over ears, not wanting to let go of a favourite toy, or even crying and screaming.

This idea is based on visual and kinaesthetic learning and helps a child calm down. It helps them think about what they want to do first of all, by providing them with a choice leaf.

Welcome the child on arrival and hold out two or three leaves with the play choices indicated. Ask them what they would like to do first from the leaf choices offered. Once a leaf is chosen, ask the child to help you stick it to the activity tree and then lead the child over to that activity.

You are not limiting the child to just that specific activity, but you are helping the transition between coming in and getting settled by helping the child to choose and reducing the overwhelming feeling of it all being too much.

Think

Some children would benefit from seeing photographs of the various activities that are on offer, others may find it easier if they are given a choice of objects to choose from such as tray offering a paint brush, a construction brick and a book.

Listening Enemies

Activity and key ideas

When we are working with young children our lives are hectic and full of activity. It is easy to lose some of our listening skills. The points below are some important listening enemies we need to be aware of.

Pretend listening

This is when a child is demanding your attention and you are trying to focus on several things. You bend down to listen to the child but in reality your mind is elsewhere and you only hear a part of the message.

Think about how you know you have been listened to:

- eye contact
- reflection of message
- action – something is done as a result of the listening.

Catch yourself pretending to listen and challenge yourself to pay attention to what the child is really trying to communicate. It often takes patience and a little more time.

Jumping ahead listening

This is about assuming we know what the child wants or is trying to say. Often we are trying to save time and speak before the child has finished their sentence. When this happens as an adult, it is frustrating; sometimes people get it wrong and it makes us feel cross. We feel undervalued and frustrated that we are not sufficiently important to warrant a bit of time to be heard. Catch yourself jumping ahead and allow the child time to express themselves.

Basing your listening on past experience

We can often name specific children who are likely to be associated to incidents in our settings. However, be aware of basing your listening on this experience. Each time an incident takes place, look at it from a new perspective. It is not necessarily what you think …

'Mrs Usher, Mrs Usher, Rhea's broken the blackboard!'
'OK Jessica, thank you for telling me.'
A few seconds later, Mrs Usher realises that Rhea is not in today, and she has based her listening on past experience!

Be aware of other children manipulating what you hear.

Tone of Voice and Body Language

Activity and key ideas

Whatever we say or however we behave in front of children we are giving them permission to do the same. Young children learn by copying and we need to be role models to promote positive language and positive behaviour.

It is important to help children understand how a person's tone of voice and language indicates their emotions and feelings. The children will also begin to recognise what your tone of voice means in relation to how you are feeling.

Game

Tell the children they are going to pretend to be an animal. Let the children choose one animal they want to be and practise the animal sounds and movements.

Imagine the children have chosen to be a duck. Tell a story about a duck. During the story the duck has lost a toy and needs to quack very sadly. He finds that someone has taken the toy and quacks very crossly. He then finds his toy again and quacks happily. Experiment with happy, cross and sad waddling movements. Children love this game and enjoy playing in character.

Play with different characters and work within the children's own choices. Allow the children to continue the game and choose further animals. This is good practice to support teamwork and team decision making.

Think

Use the ideas and actions as replacement behaviour for children who are feeling angry or cross. Instead of hitting another child, get them to act out their anger like a duck or crocodile.

Echolalic Language and Echopraxic Behaviour

Activity and key ideas

Some children may not have the ability to use their own words to express themselves so instead will 'borrow' language from others. This may be repeating exactly what you have said or may be repeating something they have heard from a previous conversation, television or audio medium. This is known as *echo* (copying) *lalic* (language) behaviour.

Echopraxia, also known as *echokinesis* is the involuntary repetition or imitation of another person's actions.

Case study 1

Anna's teacher says to Anna, 'Hi, time to tidy up now, OK?' Anna repeats back to her teacher, 'Hi, time to tidy up now, OK?' A little while later the teacher returns and Anna is still playing. The teacher is cross because she thought Anna knew she was meant to tidy up, however, Anna was only repeating what the teacher had said.

Do we know the children have understood? Ask the child to *show you* what they are meant to be doing.

Case study 2

Two children are fighting over a toy and one child begins to kick. While you are sorting this out, Sam stands up and begins to kick his chair. Is this poor behaviour, or is Sam exhibiting echopraxic behaviour?

Activity

When asking a child to complete an action such as tidying up, ask them to *tell* you what they need to do next. The child will need to process the question and respond rather than just copy your language. Now ask the child to *show* you what they need to do now. Illustrate by helping to put away the first two toys or items, the child may then use their echopraxic behaviour to copy your actions.

Think

If you notice inappropriate echopraxic behaviour, offer an alternative behaviour such as an action song for the child to copy instead to distract them and settle them back down.

Hi, time to tidy up now, OK?

Using Visual Structure – A Quick Introduction

As mentioned earlier the majority of children are visual and kinaesthetic learners yet we live in a verbal world. It is not always easy for a child to interpret and process language and make sense of what is being said. We need to support children's ability to listen, comprehend and respond verbally. With this in mind, it is important when we speak to children to reinforce our verbalisation by using visual clues.

We are surrounded by visual stimuli all the time and use facial expressions, body language and gestures without thinking about it. All these give others clues about what we are trying to communicate. However, some children need more than this. They need visual structure to help decode the spoken word. It is especially important if the child is very young, has English as a second language or has a communication difficulty such as autism.

What is simple visual structure?

Objects of reference – these are things that can be held up to provide a clue such as a pair of shoes when asking a child to get their shoes on or a lunch box when telling a child to line up for lunchtime. They can be used when giving a child a choice of what they would like to do by offering a series of objects such as a wooden spoon for baking, a paintbrush for art or a piece of track for playing trains.

Visual images – these are useful for children who need to know what is happening next or need a little help in self-organising. They usually consist of a series of images, pictures, symbols or photographs indicating what happens through a passage of time. It is advisable that no more than three or four images are used at once and some children can only work within the context of 'now' and 'then'.

toilet   wash hands   dry hands

Widgit Symbols © Widgit Software 2002–2015 www.widgit.com

Visual images can also be used to support the child to indicate choice, to help a child sequence and to support the understanding of social integration and appropriate social behaviour.

Body language and gestures – children take additional cues from body language. A child may recognise an emotion from a facial expression or understand you want to be given something when holding out your hand. Remember to make your body language as open and positive as possible. It is easy to accidentally shut a child off by using poor body language.

Visual structures are important during times of transition and change, especially where the child may not know exactly what to expect, where they are meant to be or what they are meant to be doing.

Other forms of visual structure are available including IT solutions such as Apps or computer programs.

There are many ways to use visual structure creatively; this section contains just a few simple ideas. The challenge is for you to think from the child's perspective and consider how else visual structure can be used to best support the child.

Making a Simple Visual Schedule Board

Resources needed

Thick card 30 x 21cm (A4 size)
Sticky tape
Pictures, symbols or photographs
Hook and loop tape
Laminator if available

Activity and key ideas

Most visual boards display symbols in a straight line from left to right. However, some children may prefer to work from top to bottom. If this is the case turn the display board to use it vertically.

Before you begin think carefully about what you want to convey to the child. This example uses a sequence of putting toys away before lunchtime. If the child is deeply engaged in play and we ask them to put their game away, it could be frustrating and the child may not want to comply. By using a visual schedule board the child knows why the instruction is being given and what is going to happen next. Consider the actions you want to convey in order of sequence and keep the instructions as simple as possible:

1. Put toys away
2. Line up
3. Lunchtime.

Making the board

Take a sheet of thick A4 card, place it in a landscape orientation and fold it into three equal sections creating a triangular prism shape. Stick a length of loop tape along two of the faces and then tape the two long sides together so it holds the shape by itself.

Making the communication tiles

Use whatever images you have chosen that the child recognises and relates to. Symbol programs are available to purchase for use on your own computer, free clip art is readily available, photographs can be taken or your own images may be drawn. Cut the images into squares approximately 5–6 cm and laminate them to give extra strength. Stick a small piece of hook tape onto the reverse of each card so they can be attached to the display board.

Think

If the child is already using symbols make sure you use the same ones. It is important to create continuity for the child and not to confuse them with too many different images that mean the same thing.

Some children need to see that they have completed a task. If this is the case, add a pocket to the board marked 'Done'. Each time a task has been completed take the tile from the board and put it into the pocket.

Remember – KISS
Keep It Super Simple!

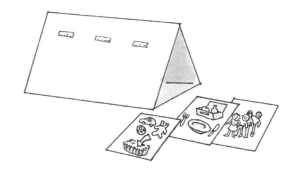

Creating a Visual Clock-Face Timetable

Resources needed

Thick card 30 x 21cm (A4 size)
A split pin
Marker pens
Hook and loop tape
Pictures, symbols or photographs

Activity and key ideas

Some children worry about what is going to happen next. This idea simply allows the child to understand what is happening during the day.

Before you begin, note down what you want to achieve on the visual clock and what will be happening during the course of the day. For example, you may want to divide it into the following segments:

- Welcome
- Indoor play
- Choose
- Snack
- Outdoor play
- Lunchtime
- Carpet time
- Home time.

Cut a large circle from the card. Use a marker pen to divide it into however many segments are necessary for your clock timetable. Starting at the top and following around clockwise, paste a picture, symbol or photograph to indicate the activity in each segment.

Cut an arrow shape from card. Make sure that is long enough to point at the timetable images but not cover them. Make a small hole

in the centre of the card and use the split pin to attach the arrow to the front of the clock face.

Each time you move from one activity or session to the next, ask a child in your setting to turn the arrow onto the next segment. Use the clock face to help explain to the children why they need to pack up their toys or get ready for the next activity.

Think
Some older children may like to have the times indicated on the segments so they can compare the visual clock-face timetable to a real clock.

Widgit Symbols © Widgit Software 2002–2015 www.widgit.com

Creating a Simple Now/Then Board

Resources needed

Thick card 21 x 15cm (A5 size)
Pens
Hook and loop tape
Picture images

Activity and key ideas

Young children or those who have a communication difficulty may need to have a simplified communications board.

To create a simple board divide the card into 4 equal sections. Draw a box on the first and third sections and label these 'now' (left-hand box) and 'then' (right-hand box). In the second and forth sections attach pieces of loop tape so these appear to the right of each box.

Use the visual tiles you have previously made to indicate to the child what is going to happen next.

Widgit Symbols © Widgit Software 2002–2015 www.widgit.com

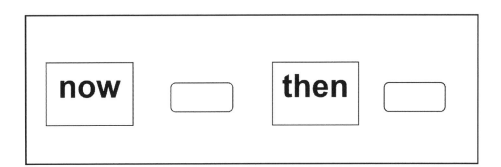

To Finish Later Box

Resources needed

Large attractive basket or box

Large label

Activity and key ideas

Some children get frustrated because they have not finished what they are doing. If the child is asked to put away their half-made construction or jigsaw they feel that their work is not important and it can lower self-esteem and confidence levels. This can result in actions which could be seen as poor behaviour.

Instead create a simple 'To finish later' basket. Use an attractive basket or box that can be placed in a specific area and stick a large label marked 'To finish later' on the front.

Always support the child to put unfinished items in the box themselves so that they know they can go back to the project another time. When the child returns to free-choice play, always offer the half-finished project first. If they don't want to complete it, the rule is that it gets put back into general circulation for all children to access. This way you will not end up with lots of half-finished projects.

Think

If the project or play activity has to be put away, take a digital photograph of it first of all so the child has a record of what they have achieved and can still feel good about themselves. Create a display on the wall for everyone to see labelled 'Look what we have done'.

Create a Visual Choice Board

Resources needed

Thick card 21 x 15cm (A5 size)
A split pin
Hook and loop tape
Pictures, symbols or photographs
Laminator if available

Activity and key ideas

I have already mentioned that some children find choice hard, especially when faced with too much choice. This idea helps the child see what choices they have by using a visual choice board.

To make the board, draw three triangular segments onto the card to create spaces on which to attach three 'choice' images. Stick a small piece of loop tape onto each segment.

Cut a small arrow from thick card and use a split pin to fix it through the card above the central segment. Ensure the arrow is long enough to point to each segment but not to cover the images.

Take photographs, use symbols or draw your own images to represent the play choices that the child has. Limit the choice initially to three options. Cut the images out, stick onto card and laminate. Stick a piece of hook tape onto the back of the choice cards.

Ask the child which activity they would like to do *first*. Then ask the child to move the pointer arrow to indicate their choice.

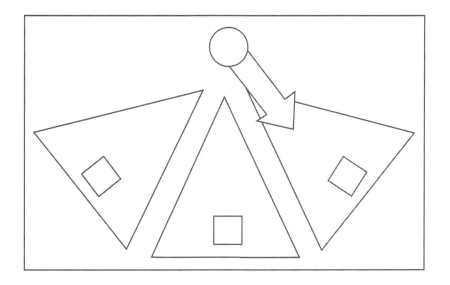

Creating Visual Rules

Resources needed

Large pieces of paper

Coloured marker pens

Pictures, symbols or photographs

Activity and key ideas

Children are asked to abide by rules all the time but do they know what the rules mean and are the rules positive? Visual rules are an excellent way of reminding children of what they *can* do, rather than constantly telling them what they cannot do.

Think about some simple rules for your setting, for example: Feet are for walking, running and jumping. Write the rule onto the paper and illustrate each section with a visual image (feet walking, a child running and a child jumping).

In a situation where a child is about to kick someone, quickly say, 'Hey, what are feet for? Let's go and have a look!'

Take the child over to the wall where the rule is displayed. Help the child tell you what the rule is and ask them if feet are for kicking another child. The visual structure will help the child understand appropriate and acceptable behaviour.

Think

Think of things that happen within the setting and, rather than creating 'no' rules, consider what children are *able* to do. Examples include:

- Hands are for holding, drawing and making
- Teeth are for smiling and eating
- Slippers are for wearing inside
- The sofa is for sitting and lying down
- Toys are for sharing.

Toys are for sharing

Positive Visual Social Reinforcement

Resources needed

Photographs, symbols or visual images

Case study

Amy is 3 years old and attends a local pre-school. At lunchtime one of the workers is overheard praising her, 'Well done Amy, I am really pleased with you!' Another worker who wanted to reinforce the positive behaviour said to Amy, 'Wow, it was good to hear you being praised. What did you do?' Amy looked up at the second worker with a huge grin and said, 'I don't know!'

It is easy to assume that children understand what they are being praised for and we give stickers to reward positive behaviour, but is there anything to remind the children what they have done well?

Activity and key ideas

Everyone understands the need to reinforce positive behaviour. However, for some children verbal reinforcement is not sufficient. We need to help the child understand what they have done well by showing them and encouraging them to continue to behave in a positive manner.

Create a series of flash cards using photographs, symbols or visual images that help to tell the child what they have done well for instance, 'Good lining up', 'Good listening', 'Good sitting'. Each time the child is praised for a specific behaviour, reinforce it by praising the child and showing them the picture at the same time. Follow up by rewarding the child with a sticker.

Think

Sometimes we concentrate our praise on children whose behaviour needs extra support. We forget other children in our setting whose behaviour is generally good all the time. If you are rewarding an individual child rather than the group think about creating an individual reward book rather than giving a public reward so other children don't get jealous of the praise given.

Making Concepts Visual – Waiting

Resources needed

A clock with clear numbers and with any plastic covering removed from the front of the clock so that you can access the clock hands
Small coloured stickers

Activity and key ideas

All children find waiting frustrating; they live a world that is in the here and now. The future seems too far away to acknowledge. We know this because they start to ask, 'Are we there yet?' before the car has even left the driveway!

Difficult behaviour often happens at times when children are bored or don't know how long they have to wait. Electronic or sand timers are an excellent way to help with this, indicating the passage of time in a very visual way. They can be carried around easily in a bag or pocket. However, if you want something a little more permanent, and something that will help the child to eventually tell the time, use a numbered clock.

The idea is to place two stickers on a clock. One on the minute hand and one on the clock face itself. When the minute-hand sticker matches or covers the clock-face sticker it is time for change.

If a change or transition is happening on the hour and the child is anxiously waiting, give them something tangible to watch. At 2.30pm place a coloured sticker onto the end of the minute hand and another above the 12. When the two stickers meet and match that is the time for transition. This gives a 30-minute warning of change.

If the change is happening at a quarter past the hour, place the sticker on the minute hand at 3.10pm and another sticker on the 3, giving a 5-minute warning. Adapt according to the individual situation.

Making Concepts Visual – Hot Spots

Resources needed

A large circle cut from a brightly coloured plastic table cloth

Activity and key ideas

What do 'here', 'there', and 'wait here a minute' mean to a young child? Where exactly is 'here'? Such concepts are hard to grasp at the best of times, and even more so if the child is confused, upset or anxious.

This idea uses a simple circle cut from plastic that can be folded up, put into your pocket and used whenever it is needed as your 'hot spot'. Suggestions for using your hot spot include:

- when starting a line, put the hot spot on the ground and it becomes the front of the line
- when asking a child to wait 'here', put the hot spot on the ground and it becomes 'here'
- when starting a game the beginning of the race starts from the hot spot
- when asking a child to have time out, the hot spot becomes the standing still space.

Hot spots can be used in many different ways including to praise or reward good behaviour. For example, ask the child to stand on your hot spot to be awarded a sticker or behaviour medal. It becomes a special place that emphasises the praise awarded.

Responding to Kinaesthetic Learners

So far we have concentrated on visual structures, but many children need to touch, move and do as well as see. This section focuses on activities that involve the child in physical activities that promote positive behaviour. Many of these also use visual structure.

Always use language when working with children, we live in a verbal world and the child needs to learn and understand what language means. Use the ideas contained in this section to reinforce positive behaviour but keep language clear and simple and don't use too many sentences or instructions at any one time.

Always think from the child's perspective and ask yourself the question, 'Do the children understand what I am trying to say?'

Music and Movement

Activity and key ideas

Children respond well to a regular beat which can be offered through music and movement. This can be particularly useful when waiting, lining up, tidying up and at times of transition.

Choose a tune that is familiar to the child for instance, *Here We Go Round the Mulberry Bush*. Instead of singing the usual words, create words that help the children understand what they are meant to be doing. For example:

Here we go round and pick up toys, pick up toys, pick up toys,
Here we go round and pick up toys and put them in the toy bin.

Follow on with other verses:

This is the way we all line up, all line up, all line up.
This is the way we all line up, standing in a row.

Think
Ask the children to make up their own words and develop songs and movements to use in your setting using tunes that are familiar to them.

Lining-up Games

Activity and key ideas

Standing in a queue to pay at a supermarket can be frustrating for adults but even more so for a child who has little patience and wants whatever is going to happen to happen NOW! Yet, during childhood standing in line is an important skill and teaches the child polite behaviour that will be used throughout their lives.

The task of lining up is harder for some than others, but all children can benefit from these ideas.

Pass the hat

This game relies upon imagination. The first child starts by putting an imaginary hat on their head, then takes it off and passes it to the next child. While the hat is travelling down the line the first child runs to the back of the line and everyone moves forward one place.

The next child pretends to put on a coat and again this movement travels down the line with this first child moving to the back of the line. The game continues with various imaginary actions. The children feel as though they are moving forward in the line as they step forward even if it is only into the place vacated by the first child.

Chinese whispers – in movements

In a similar way to the previous game, the first child starts a movement which is sent as a chain down the line. This could be a rhythmic hand clap, turning in a circle, blinking, rubbing their tummy or any other movement that does not require the child to move away from the line. Once the movement has started down the line the first child runs to the back, everyone takes a step forward and the next child begins another movement.

This activity requires the children to concentrate on what is going to happen next, there is an element of surprise and the children do not get bored.

Counting games

Choose a rhyme that is familiar to the child for instance, *One, Two, Buckle My Shoe* and add actions to go alongside the words:
One, two, buckle my shoe (the first two children shout out their numbers and all children bend down to pretend to tie their shoes)
Three, four, knock on the door (the third and fourth children shout out their numbers and all children pretend to knock on the door).
Continue until you get to:
Nine, ten, start again! (the ninth and tenth children shout out their numbers and all children join in with, 'start again!').

Counting games for older children

Ask the children to count themselves with each child saying their number out loud.
Ask the children to count themselves backwards, starting with the highest number first and counting down.
Ask the children to count up in even and then in odd numbers.

Spatial Awareness

Resources needed

Something to denote a defined space such as:

String

Hula hoops

Carpet squares

Masking tape

Activity and key ideas

Children like to touch. This is very much part of learning and is essential to the child's development. However, it becomes difficult when touch is not invited and it irritates other children and becomes offensive.

We have all seen the child, who cannot stop themselves from fiddling with the child's hair in front, who pulls someone's jumper or just prods someone to see what happens! This can lead to upsets and frustration when personal space invaded, eventually leading to anger which is communicated by response behaviour.

Spatial awareness is hard to teach. How do you know when it is socially acceptable to stand near to someone, or to know that you are too near?

Some children need the boundaries to be physical so they can 'see' and 'feel' their own space. The ideas below may help.

- Give each child a hula hoop at story time. They are only to sit inside their hoop and must not touch anyone else in another hoop.
- Create a set of circles using the string on the floor. The same rules apply as above.

- Use different coloured carpet squares to donate space and place. These can also be useful to help particular children contribute when others tend to interrupt. For example ask, 'Put your hand up to answer this question *only* if you are sitting on a *blue* carpet square.' Make sure everyone is included but the activity can help those that normally don't get a chance to contribute.
- Use masking tape to donate a space on a table or desk. We often see children sneaking a pencil away from another child which eventually causes a breakdown in behaviour. By indicating space and place clearly, it helps the children to know where they can put their belongings and to keep to their own space and not invade others.

Using Your Hands to Indicate Choice

Activity and key ideas

If the child is behaving in a way that requires intervention consider what choices the child has. Make the choice simple by holding out your hands and putting one forward as you give the choices for example:

(Holding out your left hand) 'You can sit nicely and finish your lunch,' or (holding out your right hand), 'You can get down from the table and wait until everyone else is finished.'

Ask the child what they want to do by offering your hands and by doing so inviting them to touch your hands to indicate their choice. If the child is not responding, repeat again using the same words.

If the child touches your left hand, then immediately praise the child by saying, 'Good choice, well done.' If the child touches your right hand, follow through with the consequence to the behaviour.

If the child does not respond and comply to your request, then put out your right hand and say, 'OK, you have chosen to sit in the corner because you did not sit nicely and finish your lunch as I asked.'

The consequence of the behaviour needs to be appropriate and agreed within the setting. The example given is just that, an example.

Think

The consequence to poor behaviour must be meaningful to the child. Don't accidentally praise poor behaviour by providing a consequence that the child wants. For example, Amir is playing up during numeracy pinching other children. The teacher intervenes saying, 'Amir, that's enough! Go and sit in the quiet area.' Actually, that is exactly what Amir wants; he has got out of doing something he did not want to do. The next time it is numeracy he has learned that all he needs to do is pinch other children to be sent out.

Using Colours to Support Children's Behaviour – Traffic Lights Game

Resources needed

Soft toys

Red, orange and green ribbons

Activity and key ideas

Ask the children to choose three soft toys or teddy bears that you have in your setting. Tie a piece of ribbon around each of the toys' necks like scarves. Use red, orange and green ribbons.

Each of the colours represents an action in a similar way to traffic lights. Red indicates 'Stop', orange indicates 'Wait and listen' and green indicates 'Go'.

Ask the children to tell you an action they can do, such as jumping, hopping or turning in a circle. Hide the bears behind your back or in a bag. Choose a bear and hold it high in the air. The children's actions are based on the colour of the bear. If the bear is wearing a red scarf they need to stop still like a statue; if orange they need to stand with their hand to their ear to listen; and if the scarf is green they can continue to move or you can choose another child to change the movement for the other children to follow.

Once the children are used to the action relating to the colour you can use the bears to help them understand appropriate behaviour:

- If the child needs to stop what they are doing, hold up the bear with the red scarf
- If the child needs to listen, hold up the bear with the orange scarf

- If the child is doing really well and you want them to carry on, hold up the bear wearing the green scarf and put your thumb up to indicate, 'Well done, good behaviour!'

Think

Think about what else you could use instead of coloured ribbons. Perhaps try making your own set of traffic lights out of card.

Replacement Activities Demonstrating Anger and Frustration

Resources needed

Plastic tablecloth

Permanent marker pen

Bucket of soft play dough (or similar)

Timer

Activity and key ideas

If a child is feeling very angry and they want to display that emotion, other children often get in the way and can get hurt.

Saying, 'No we don't behave in that way,' puts a lid on the behaviour but the child may resent the command. Eventually, the pressure of frustration and anger becomes too much and the child may display inappropriate physical behaviour.

Replacement activities for children who really do need to 'let it out' can be helpful if well managed. This works well when you know your children and can read when the child's temper is starting to rise.

I feel angry mat

Draw a set of concentric circles on the plastic tablecloth and give each ring a score with the centre being the highest score.

Place the tablecloth on the floor (preferably outside) and away from other children. Provide the child who is angry with a bucket of soft dough and allow the child to pick up a handful of dough and throw it at the mat.

Once the child has had a few goes and has released their immediate anger, begin to draw them into a game by asking if they can hit the middle of the mat or a specific ring to score points.

Take turns with the child and use humour to help them come out of their temper. Tell the child that you are really good at this game and can always score a bullseye. Throw the play dough and miss on purpose. If the child is a better aim than you their self-esteem and confidence may begin to grow. Invite the child to laugh at your poor aim.

Think

Think of other activities that you could introduce as replacements to poor behaviour which relate to the movements the child is exhibiting. For example, a child who likes to kick may value an opportunity to kick a ball at a target, kick leaves or bounce on a trampoline. A child who pulls other people's hair may value a piece of elastic that they can pull and manipulate.

When providing replacement activities, always tell the child that there is a time limit and use a timer. If this is not done, the child may spend the entire session taking their frustration out on the activity when you want them to join back in and learn how to control their temper.

Behaviour-Safe Places (Dens and Tents)

Resources needed
Small pop-up tent or other safe space such as a large sheet spread over a table to create a den
Soft blankets
Soft toys
Soft-play items

Activity and key ideas
None of us want to see our children stressed and angry, it makes us sad and we want to take it all away. The majority of time we can cajole, change the activity or provide a replacement kinaesthetic behaviour.

Sometimes none of this works, especially if the child is hurting over something that we have no control over such as parents splitting up, a bereavement or a situation where the child feels they have lost something, such as a new baby (loss of attention), house move (loss of security), or a new school (loss of friends). In these cases we cannot take away the pain, but need to support the child by providing a safe area in which they can display their feelings.

As adults we can take a walk, have a hot bath, or do something physical like running or swimming to de-stress. Children don't always have this ability to self-regulate how they respond to stress.

If you are working with a child who is angry at the world, recognise the anger by saying, 'I know you are feeling bad. If you want to show how angry you are that's OK, but only if you use the angry tent.'

Place lots of soft toys, blankets, inflatable and soft-play items in the tent. If the child wants to hit out at the world it is fine to do so in that safe environment. Be aware of other children wanting to join in. Tell them that today this is Zoe's special place. If they want to play in there another day they can.

Think
Don't have the tent out every day or the child may become too reliant on it. Try to use a range of techniques to allow the children to express their emotions.

Recognising Emotions and Expressions

Case study

Raja is 3 years old. He enjoys being with other children; he loves laughing and running around. He does not recognise it when others are upset with him. He has difficulty understanding facial expressions. If he has annoyed another child and they frown at him, he laughs. If he sees something he wants he takes it and does not recognise how the other child may be feeling. This behaviour can cause friction and misunderstanding.

This case study may seem familiar. Many children have difficulty in empathising with others and understanding emotions and expressions. It is important to help teach children understand how others are feeling to help them understand how their own behaviour affects other children.

This section concentrates on activities that help children to learn to appreciate the feelings of others and understand how their own actions may make someone else feel sad or happy.

Some of the ideas in this section are based on the use of a story. Please feel free to use the story below or adapt and write your own.

Example story – *Mrs Pig's New Pink Jumper*

Mrs Pig was looking for her new pink jumper. She looked up, she looked down, she looked round and round. It was not there. Then she noticed Mr Pig had put her new pink jumper in the garden on the scarecrow. Mrs Pig frowned. Mrs Pig pushed out her bottom lip. Mrs Pig screwed up her eyes. She felt CROSS and she stamped her foot. In fact, Mrs Pig was so cross she felt ANGRY!

Mr Pig came into the house and saw Mrs Pig. 'Why are you frowning?' he said. 'Why is your bottom lip out, and why are your eyes all screwed up, and why are you stamping your foot?'

Mrs Pig huffed and puffed, she crossed her arms and she stamped her foot again. She was so cross she couldn't whisper; she couldn't talk quietly in her indoor voice. She was so cross she needed to shout. 'Why have you used my new pink jumper on your scarecrow?' she shouted.

Mr Pig looked confused and sad. He was worried that Mrs Pig was angry. 'I haven't,' he said and a tear drop ran from his eye. He wiped it away. 'Don't be angry with me. Look your new pink jumper is on the back of the pink chair!'

'Ohhhhhhhhhh,' said Mrs Pig. She felt very sorry. She had been angry at Mr Pig and he had not taken her jumper. 'If that is my jumper what is on the scarecrow?' she asked.

Mr Pig laughed, he was happy. Mrs Pig was not angry any more. 'It's my old pink pyjamas,' he said. Mrs Pig began to smile. She did not frown. She did not stick out her bottom lip. She did not screw up her eyes. Instead she opened her mouth, her lips curled up at the edges and she began to laugh and laugh and laugh. She laughed so hard that she began to cry.

'Oh, Mr Pig,' she said, 'I am so sorry. I blamed you for something you had not done.' 'That's OK,' said Mr Pig, 'I'm happy that you are happy. Let's have a cup of tea.' So that is just what they did.

Find the Emotion Face

Resources needed

Mrs Pig's New Pink Jumper story (see page 33)
Large, coloured pieces of paper
Coloured pens

Activity and key ideas

Start by drawing a series of simple emotion expression faces onto large pieces of paper. If you are following our story, make the faces piggy faces. Begin simply for younger children and include happy, sad and angry. For older children add more subtle expressions, such as confused, frightened and worried.

There are plenty of expression faces available to download and print from free clip art programmes if you prefer. Think carefully about what coloured paper you are using to display an emotion face. Sad is generally depicted as blue, happy as green and angry as red.

Spread the pieces of paper around the room. Tell the children a simple story such as *Mrs Pig's New Pink Jumper* and ask them to undertake the actions including the emotional expressions. Exaggerate the expressions and ask the children to copy you. When you use an emotional expression word such as 'angry' or 'happy' the children need to run to the correct face and sit beside it.

Think

If working with older children, talk about the story and ask if they have ever had similar emotions such as angry, confused, sad, sorry and happy. Make up your own stories using these emotions.

Emotion Masks

Resources needed

Mrs Pig's New Pink Jumper story (see page 33)
Paper plates
Scissors
Coloured pens
Straws or lollipop sticks

Activity and key ideas

Draw a series of simple faces onto the paper plates. Stick the plates onto straws or lollipop sticks so that the children can hold them up.

Re-tell the story of *Mrs Pig's New Pink Jumper* or make up one of your own. Ask the children to show you the correct plate for the emotion expressed.

To develop understanding, expand the story and add in new emotions. You could also ask the children to act out the story using the plates as masks.

Think

Provide the children with a series of statements and ask them to show you how the person might be feeling using the plates. Examples include:

- Jason felt ... when Dane kicked him
- Amy felt ... when Japhed shared his toys with her
- Naomi felt ... when she lost her teddy.

Expand this idea by adding in movements that would help to show the feeling.

Mirroring an Emotion

Resources needed

Mrs Pig's New Pink Jumper story (see page 33)
Plastic safety mirrors
Write-on/wipe-off pens
Soft cloths

Activity and key ideas

Tell the children the story of Mrs Pig or make up one of your own. As you tell the story ask the children to draw a facial expression onto the mirror such as 'happy'. When they have done this ask them to hold the mirror up to their face. Ask them to try to replicate the same face as the one they have drawn. Wipe-off the drawing with the cloth and continue with the story, drawing new expressions and practising facial expressions in the mirrors.

Place two children facing each other. See if they can 'mirror' the other child's expression and guess what it means.

Case study

Heather was making a cross face in the mirror. She turned to her teacher and said, 'Nathan looked like that.' Her teacher asked, 'When did you see Nathan looking like that?' Heather replied, 'Just after I bit him.'

Use the children's conversations and comments to explore feelings and what behaviours relate to which emotions.

Think

Take this a bit further and begin to think about how the children can help to change other people's emotions. What could you do to make someone else happy or pleased? Perhaps by sharing a toy or inviting another child to play? Change the expressions on the mirrors according to what the children say.

Take photos of the children's expressions. Create a wall display alongside simple line drawings demonstrating simple emotions.

Feeling the Emotions

Resources needed

Plastic play tray

Soft play dough

Flour

Sand

Shaving foam

Additional messy play resources

Activity and key ideas

This is a fun and messy activity to explore facial expressions and emotions.

Create a series of facial expressions in the play tray using soft play dough. Manipulate the dough to create happy, sad and cross faces.

Fill the tray with flour, sand or shaving foam and ask the children to draw your facial expressions using their fingers.

Think

Don't do this activity in isolation. Always demonstrate the emotion using your own facial expressions and ask the children to copy. Ask the children to recognise other children's facial expressions and help them to recognise how others may be feeling.

This task may not be easy for a child on the autism spectrum who does not readily read facial expressions. Research and print out photographs of people expressing various emotions (*Talk about ... Emotions* published by Yellow Door offers a printed and digital bank of facial expressions). Explore with the child exactly what is happening to the face and the changes and differences that occur with each emotion. Ask the child to try and replicate the facial features in drawings or models.

Ideas to Support Anxieties About Separation, Abandonment and Attachment Which Can Result in Emotional Behaviour

Worry and anxiety is a common feature of children's behaviour. Fear is a major feature within this. It is hard for a child to be separated from a parent when going into a setting. This can cause varying degrees of behaviour from a few tears that are short lived, through to such stress that the setting becomes worried about the child's mental health. It does not help that parents may feel guilty and upset that their child is crying, and indeed the parents themselves may not want to let go.

This section has various ideas to support anxieties about both separation and abandonment anxiety, and also considers separation to a specific attachment such as a cuddle blanket.

No one idea will work in isolation. It will probably be necessary to find a series of ideas to put together to support the individual child or young person. Always take a child-centred approach and think about the situation from their viewpoint.

Separation and Smells

Resources needed

A collection of items that provide smells that are familiar to the child

Activity and key ideas

Smell is a surprisingly strong sense and is one that the young child quickly learns to use in the first stages of their lives. A baby knows if they are being held by their mum or someone they trust. The person smells right and they have the added confidence of the hold and the recognition of voice.

It is comforting getting home from holiday, opening your own front door and walking into your home that smells familiar. We all have a personal smell. It is made up from many aspects of our lives. It includes the washing powder we use, the shampoo or soap we use, our deodorant, the perfume we wear and even our sweat.

Children who have separation anxiety can be supported via scents.

Ideas you could use:

- Work with the parent and ask them to provide the setting with something that holds a familiar scent of mum or dad such as a scarf. You could add a few drops of a familiar scent they wear regularly. Use the scarf when picking up and holding young children and babies. Swap the scarf between workers so that the child does not develop an attachment to one specific staff member.
- Borrow a cardigan or jumper and if the child is really upset allow them to wrap themselves up in something familiar.

- If mum uses a specific soap, shampoo or deodorant, have the same scent in the setting. Use it to wash your hands, or spray onto your clothes so the child feels comforted by smelling something familiar.

Think

Explain to the parent what you are trying to achieve and send home any bedding that needs washing so the child is comfortable with the familiar smell of home-washed linen.

Welcoming the Child for the First Time

Resources needed

Favourite toys
Prepared stickers/badge

Activity and key ideas

If you are aware that there may be anxiety issues before the child attends the setting or if the child is transferring to your setting from somewhere else, preparation is the key to help the child feel secure. This is particularly important if you know that the child has any underlying impairment or condition such as autism.

Find out as much about the child as possible. Identify favourite activities and toys and particularly if there are any obsessions or special interests with toys, objects, characters from books, television or games.

On the first day the child is due to arrive, welcome the child wearing a large badge displaying the child's special interest. Give them a pre-printed sticker with an image of the special interest and if possible have a toy ready that the child will associate with. Use a familiar character sticker over their coat hook so they feel comfortable.

Prepare a range of activities that all children can participate in associated with the special interest. For example, if the child is interested in trains then create a crafts activity around making trains. Some children who are literal thinkers may require something more specific, such as pictures of *Thomas the Tank Engine* to stick onto cardboard boxes to make trains. Rather than just making 'a train' they need to make 'Thomas'.

Think about other activities that can encourage creative play, and learning objectives using the special interest as a catalyst to involvement. For example:

- introduce models and plastic characters of the special interest into messy play
- create special interest counters to support numeracy
- use models in storytelling
- use mask making to lead to music and movement activities
- create a tidy up song using any special characters' names.

Think

Remember that the child will eventually need to reduce their reliance on special interests to fully participate in other activities. Be selective in how you use their special interest.

Put Mum in the Diary ... and on the Clock!

Resources needed

Schedule board (see page 16)

Clock-face schedule board (see page 17)

Photograph of mum or principal carer

Activity and key ideas

One of the scariest things for a child is when they do not know what is going to happen next. The majority of their lives are adult led. Adults make decisions for them, when they will eat, when they get taken out, when they go to nursery, an early years setting or school. We ask children to trust us all the time, without question.

When a child has separation anxiety, they are questioning our decisions and have unanswered questions of their own. Will I ever see Mum again? Will I stay here forever? Will I go home? Many of these questions remain unasked and unanswered. However, a child's behaviour is a form of communication and perhaps it is the behaviour that makes you think the questions are there.

What can we do to reassure the child that mum or dad will be back? Consider the previous section on using visual structure. If you are using a schedule board, then at the end of the day add in a picture of mum and home. This simple step can help the child through the day. Each time they get upset show them the schedule board and what they will be doing. Always finish with a picture of mum. This reassures the child that after they have done the various activities, mum will be there to pick them up.

When working with older children use the clock-face schedule board idea and add on a photograph of the parent at the time they are due to pick up the child. If the child gets upset during the day, reassure them that their mum/dad will be back later and show them the photograph. Refer to all the activities that need to be done before they come back.

Dependent upon the child, 15–30 minutes before the parent or carer is due to arrive, show the child a smaller schedule board with various small tasks to keep them occupied. This will help the child to be busy and not standing by the door crying. It is important for both the child and parent to see each other at the end of the day in a happy state. If the child is upset the parent may get upset which means the next day's separation will be even harder.

Reassure the parent that the child has had a good day. If possible take some simple digital photos of the child enjoying themselves and give to the child to show mum or dad.

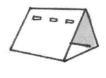   

Pictures Tell a Thousand Words

Resources needed

Photographs taken at home

Photographs of the child enjoying activities at the setting

Small album or book to stick photos into

Activity and key ideas

If a child is distressed in the mornings prior to getting to the setting and is anxious about leaving mum/dad, ask the parents to help prepare the child for the day at home.

Encourage the parent to use a simple photographic schedule on the fridge such as the child having breakfast, then sitting in the car and a further photograph of the setting itself.

Before the child begins to get upset at the fear of separation, give them a small photo book to look at. This can be viewed at home or on the journey to the setting. Display pictures of the child undertaking various activities at the setting they have enjoyed and talk about the things they like doing.

Once at the setting if the child begins to become upset give them something that is personal to the parent that needs to be given back at the end of the day. This could be a key on a chain or an identity card with the parent's picture. It will be reassuring that the item has to be given back so the child knows that mum/dad will be returning.

Think

If we are not careful the 'special item' can become an obsession, or the child may be frightened of losing it. Create a small box with the child's name on that sits in a draw or on a shelf so the child can see it and knows the item will remain safe until it is time to go home.

Who is in Today? Board

Resources needed

A large piece of card

Marker pens

Red card or paper cut into a star shape

Photographs of staff members

Hook and loop tape

Activity and key ideas

Sometimes children's anxiety on entering a setting is not about separation but is about being scared of what is happening next without the reassuring presence of someone the child trusts.

Trust can take time to build so it can be helpful for the child to have a visual image of which adults are going to be in today to help them if they need it.

It is also important to ensure the child does not build too close an attachment to any one staff member because if that person is ill or on holiday the child's anxiety may resume. The child's special helper needs to rotate amongst staff members to ensure trust is built throughout the staff team.

Create a board indicating the days of the week. At the beginning of each day display pictures of the staff members on duty. Do this first thing, so that the pictures are displayed prior to the child arriving. If a staff member is going to be late in or is away, make sure their picture is not displayed.

Cut out a star shape from a red piece of card. When the child comes in, before they engage with any activity, take them over the board to see who their special helper is for the day. Engage with the child and get them to place their red star next to their special helper image. This reassures the child that there is someone they can trust and go to if they need to.

Think

Only display the staff photos one day at a time. If the child sees images of the staff for the next day and something happens and the staff member is not in, their expectations will not be met.

Ideas to Reduce the Reliance on a Security Blanket

Resources needed

Scissors
Needle and thread
Security blanket

Activity and key ideas

We often see young children attached to a favourite blanket that gets dragged around behind them and taken everywhere. When the child is very young this is perfectly acceptable and is reassuring for the child. As the child gets slightly older, the blanket may become a hindrance to participating in other activities or becomes socially unacceptable behaviour.

Consider what it is about the blanket that the child likes? Is it the smell, the colour, or the feel? Instead of facing complete separation anxiety by taking away the blanket, think about how you can reduce the reliance in stages. Possibilities may include:

- Cut out a large rectangle from the blanket, fold it in half and stitch up two open sides to create a pillowcase. Stuff the pillowcase with a cushion or even an old jumper and sew up the final seam. The pillow can still be hugged and cuddled but is smaller to carry around.
- Cut a rectangle off the end of the blanket. Fold in half and sew up each long side to create a pocket. The child can put their hand into the pocket and hold it up to their face to smell. It is still reassuring and is part of the blanket but can be carried around easily and can fit into their own pocket when not required. It is a partial transition stage used to eventually reduce the emotional reliance upon their security blanket.

- For older children, make part of the blanket into a pencil case. No-one need know that it is part of the security blanket but the child still has a remnant of security to hold if it is needed.
- Eventually, the child may just need a small strip of the blanket in a pocket or made into a bracelet to reassure themselves all is well.

Think

It can be useful to reduce the size of a favourite blanket at the beginning of the obsession. Cut it in two and have one for the child and one for the wash!

Using Obsessions with Objects Effectively

Resources needed

Object of interest
Photographs of the special object
Sand timer

Activity and key ideas

Many children have a special toy they are attached to. Usually children grow out of this as the world becomes an exciting place with other things to engage them. However, some children (especially those on the autism spectrum) become obsessed with certain objects that get carried around everywhere.

Case study

Finn loved his old-fashioned plunge spinner, he would carry it everywhere. When he started in his early years setting he would not let go of it and would want to play with it all the time, to the detriment of other learning. As it was an isolated activity it was not helpful in supporting him to socialise with other children.

His key worker Jenny recognised that she could not take it off him straight away as it would be too distressing. Instead she took photographs of each of the children holding their favourite toys and displayed them on a wall.

Jenny created a visual schedule board for Finn indicating what he would be doing during the day. She scheduled in several opportunities to play with the spinner but on each activity entry for the spinner she added in a picture of a sand timer.

Finn was able to play with his spinner for 5 minutes until the timer ran out and then it went back on the shelf. At this point Jenny would give Finn a laminated photograph of himself with the spinner to keep in his pocket so he knew it was his. During the day if he got upset that he couldn't have the spinner, Jenny would use the visual schedule board to show him that he could play with the spinner after he had undertaken other activities.

Over time the schedule board changed with less time offered for playing with the spinner.

Ideas to Help Calm Children Down

What happens when children feel hurt, angry or frustrated? Without intervention children often display their feelings through their behaviour. Others display their emotions by becoming upset and tearful.

This section takes a look at some ideas to help calm children down. Before you begin to put any of these ideas into practice, it is important to know as much about the child as possible. For instance, do you know if the parent uses any particular calming activities already that could be used with the child?

Case study 1

Tom would become very angry and upset if he did not know what was happening next. His anxiety would be displayed by fits of aggression followed by tears. At home his mum would use the same action song to help calm him down. Every time he became upset she would stand back and sing this song quietly to him, doing the actions.

This song became associated in Tom's mind with safety and security. Everything would be OK. He would calm down and eventually join in with the song and actions.

Case study 2

Jessica was an angry little girl. Her mother had just had a new baby and she was feeling jealous. When she started to have a tantrum her mother would distract her by simply blowing bubbles. Jessica loved playing with bubbles and the distraction worked every time.

If these techniques were known to the setting they could be replicated. Find out what is used to support the child when they are upset and if possible use a technique that is familiar to the child.

Using Action Songs and Movement

Activity and key ideas

When a child is upset and confused, hurt or angry they need to be reassured all is OK. The reassurance can be supported by something that is familiar to them that has a pattern and does not change.

Repetitive action songs are a good way to involve and engage the child and eventually they are likely to echo your sound and movements. Don't start singing directly in front of the child who is upset, it may annoy them more. Instead, stand to one side and allow the child to see you in their peripheral vision and hear you. Use open gestures and kneel or sit at their level. Offer eye contact but don't worry if the child does not look at you straight away.

Use a song that you know the child likes and enjoys joining in with. Sing quietly and when the child looks at you hold eye contact and encourage them to join in by nodding.

Suggested songs:

- *5 Little Speckled Frogs*
- *5 Little Monkeys*
- *Wind the Bobbin Up*
- *Head Shoulders, Knees and Toes*
- *A Sailor Went to Sea, Sea, Sea*
- *The Animals Went in Two by Two*

Think

Try making up your own action songs with the child before they are needed for calming purposes. Try to make the songs as funny as possible and sing them over and over again so the child knows the words and actions. When the child has been engaged in developing the song and giving you their ideas, they are more likely to join in 'their song' when stressed or upset.

Try re-wording the song so that it includes the child's name, that way the child has a sense of ownership over the activity.

Calming Colours

Resources needed

Lots of coloured fabric strips or scarves, including bright and pastel colours

Activity and key ideas

It is well known that the colours red and orange are often seen as 'aggressive' colours. We are probably familiar with the phrase 'seeing red'. In contrast there are also calming colours. These vary for each individual but tend to be pale blues and lilacs, or natural colours such as the colour of sand.

Lay out the fabric strips and ask the child to choose the ones that make them think of being happy, being sad, being angry and then being calm. Make a note of which colours are chosen for each child.

If a child is upset or angry and you are trying to calm them down, consider the environment around you. Are you taking them over to a quiet area where the sofa is bright red with big yellow posters on the walls, or is the environment calming with pastel blues and lilac colours?

Think about the colours the child chose to indicate emotion. Use these colour scarves or strips of fabric to create a quiet environment and sit with the child. Allow the child to hold and play with the fabrics while they tell you about their issues. This may help to calm them down and to be more communicative.

Think

Each child is an individual with individual preferences. Don't assume you know what colours would be good for calming – some children's choices may surprise you such as bright yellow, purple or even red!

The Power of Bubbles

Resources needed

Water
Containers
Bubble solution
Bubble wands

Extra resources to expand activity

Dark area or den
Torch
Food colouring

Have you ever sat by a river or stream and felt peaceful? There is something magical about being near water and hearing the sound of water pouring or bubbling over stones.

Most children love playing with water, it is such a versatile medium and is inviting. If a child is upset or you notice they are indicating trauma or stress, invite them to come with you to a quiet area and introduce them to bubbles.

Start by simply blowing bubbles through a bubble wand and allowing the child to watch. If the child wishes to touch the bubbles allow them to do so and encourage the child to participate in the activity.

As the child engages, encourage them to participate and blow the bubbles themselves. The activity soon draws children away from negative feelings. Work with the child to use different containers and different things to blow bubbles through and the child will soon engage.

Think

Expand the activity by blowing bubbles in a dark environment. Provide the child with a torch to shine onto the bubbles. This will enhance the rainbow of colours reflecting on the skin of the bubble.

Expand further by adding food colouring to the bubble mix – blow different bubble colours and see what happens when two bubbles collide and mix.

Painting a Personal Calming Picture

Resources needed
Warm water
Giant soft paint brushes, sponges or bristle brushes
Towel

Extra resources to expand activity
Warm oil or body lotions

Activity and key ideas
Touch can be a tricky subject. Some children throw themselves into your arms and want to be hugged and reassured. Others need their own personal space and dislike being 'crowded'. Consider the individual child and think from their point of view when undertaking this activity.

Warm water is calming. It is nice when we get into a warm bath and feel that we can relax and drift into another world.

Only do this activity if the child is comfortable with it and you have permission from parents.

Introduce the activity by asking the child to paint your arm and hands with warm water using a giant, soft paintbrush. Tell the child it feels lovely and offer to paint their arm and hand. Run the paintbrush down the child's arm using gentle massaging strokes, experiment by stippling the paintbrush across the child's hand, and ask them which sensation they like. If the child asks you to stop, do so immediately and provide the child with a towel.

If the child enjoys the sensation continue the activity. Often children will open up and talk about what is causing anxieties when they are in a calm and peaceful environment. Use the opportunity to offer a listening ear but don't ask the child too many questions. Silence is a powerful tool. It is human nature to fill a void of silence but try not to fill the void yourself as this can discourage the child from feeling free to talk.

Think
Extend this activity by using warm oil or body lotions as the painting medium (with permission).

Take a child-centred approach and be aware of any sensitivity the child may have to the activity. Be particularly aware if the child happens to have dyspraxia, autism or another condition where they have hyper or hypo sensitivity. Some children may like the activity but prefer a bristle brush or soft sponge.

Creating a Calm Down Box

Resources needed

A variety of items that engage the child and are visual and kinaesthetic:

Fiddle toys
Visual sensory toys
Ribbons and fur fabric
Feely bags such as bags filled with rice or pasta
Pin wheels that turn when blown

Extra resources to expand activity

Scented items
Happy emotion face outlines
Colouring pens, pencils or crayons

Activity and key ideas

Use this box when a child is calming down or during a difficult time such as time spent waiting.

Create a box that is full of items for the child to fiddle with, touch, feel and see. Do not include items that are noisy or loud, or that encourage the child to run around (balls or items to be thrown). Make the box or bag easy to put away and carry around.

Think

How about creating some smelly bags to go into the box such as a lavender bag, some fabrics with drops of perfume on them or even include some herbal tea bags.

If the child is old enough, include some paper and crayons for drawing. Print out some simple positive emotion faces for the child to colour the encouraging smiles.

Creating a Calming Space and Place

Resources needed

Small pop-up tent or other safe space, such as a large sheet spread over a table to create a den
Soft blankets
Fairy lights, white battery tea lights or toys that provide gentle light
Plastic mirrors
Music player with gentle music (if available)

Activity and key ideas

Note: this activity is similar to Activity 28 (see page 32) where we look at creating a den as a safe place for a child. This activity helps to support a child who has a sensory overload.

When we are stressed or upset the world seems to crowd in on us. Noises become noisier, colours are too bright, people seem to stand too close and we want to push the world away and go and hide somewhere. As an adult we may choose to go for a walk, have a bath or go somewhere to read a book.

It is hard for children in a vibrant and active setting to find somewhere quiet and calming. Some settings have sensory rooms that are designed to create a low sensory arousal space but if you are not lucky enough to have this, there are many ways of creating a calming space or place simply and cheaply, using any corner of the setting available.

It's about creating a barrier against the world. The environment does not have to cut out all noise but can provide a 'safe' space for the child. This may be in the form of a pop-up tent or homemade den that allows the child to 'hide' for a short time and calm down.

Think about the colour of the environment you are creating. Try not to use bright, vibrant colours. If using a pop-up play tent, pin up white or black sheets inside it to create a neutral environment.

Lights can be very soothing. Try hanging some small, soft-white fairy lights in the tent or display small white battery tea lights. There are also many cheap toys available that provide light; look for ones that are white, blue or pastel colours rather than bright reds and greens. Add some simple children's plastic safety mirrors to the environment to give additional reflections.

Finally, if you have the ability to do so, consider playing gentle music that is quiet and in the background.

Think

Think of the floor surface. If you have a pop-up tent it is easy to cover the floor with soft fabrics such as fur fabric or soft mats or rugs.

Creating Positive Praise

Reinforcing positive behaviour is a term we are all familiar with but how do we do it in practice?

It is easy to put a thumb up, smile and say well done, but does the child know what it is you are giving them praise for or even appreciate that a thumbs up actually means well done?

This section provides ideas for activities that think from the child's perspective to create positive praise that is meaningful to the individual.

We ask you to take a child-centred approach and adapt the ideas according to the child's own character, personality, likes/dislikes and any underlying impairment or condition they may have.

Use the Child's Interests to Praise Kinetically

Resources needed
Egg timer (or other type of timer)
Toys or items of special interest to the child
Reward stickers

Activity and key ideas
Most children will respond positively to smiles, thumbs up and social praise. Some, however, may not be very interested in social praise particularly if they are not very social themselves, such as child on the autism spectrum.

Think about how you can use the child's own special interests to praise and reward.

Case study
James is 5 years old. He has a fascination with his bright green car. If he could he would play with it 24 hours a day. When he goes to school, it is not always appropriate to play with his car so his teacher puts it high up on a windowsill.

When James has done something that is above the normal expectations and needs to be praised and rewarded, he gets given a 5-minute egg timer and his car. He happily turns the car upside down and spins the wheels until the egg timer runs out and the car has to be returned to the shelf. He also gets a reward sticker.

Think
Make sure that this type of reward is special and not for behaviour that you would expect normally. If you use this system too often it becomes expected and the child can be become anxious or upset if they are not allowed their special toy.

Personal Praise Charts

Resources needed
Small book or a set of blank cards
Praise stickers (ideally personalised)

Case study
Tindai rushed up to Mrs Usher in the playground before school had started, 'Mrs Usher, Mrs Usher,' he shouted. 'I have decided that today I am going to be very naughty!' 'Oh!' said Mrs Usher. 'Thank you for telling me. Any particular reason? 'Yes!' said Tindai, 'If I am naughty this morning, after lunch I can be good and you will give me a sticker.'

Not a good start to the day but an excellent learning point! It is easy for us to concentrate on the children who need a little more help in recognising good behaviour. We often try to praise them publicly by giving stickers or exaggerating our praise. However, is the behaviour we are praising anything above our expectations from any other child? Do other children feel that is it fair that the child who has poor behaviour gets praised when they do something they should be doing anyway?

Activity and key ideas
Make a personal praise chart that is between yourself and the child. Instead of offering public praise that may make others children jealous, praise the child individually. Allow them to complete a private sticker chart or small positive praise book.

Stickers can also be stuck onto blank playing cards. Each time the child does something that deserves praise, provide them with a sticker and a blank card. Eventually the cards can be made up into a set of playing cards where the stickers act as the pictures for a game of snap or pairs.

When the praise chart in whatever form it takes is complete, the child can have a reward that is appropriate to them. This may be a public sticker, extra time with their favourite toy or whatever is appropriate on an individual basis. Make it meaningful to the child.

Think
Some children will respond better to a sticker if it represents their special interest.

Reinforcing the Positive Behaviour

Resources needed

Photographs or images that show good behaviour/skills
Blank stickers

Activity and key ideas

Do children always know what they are being praised for?

Search online and find clip art or images of children doing things that you want children in your setting to replicate. Examples include: sitting down, standing in line, listening or working nicely. Symbols are also available from various software packages.

Print the images onto stickers and use them as praise stickers. This way the child feels good that they have been rewarded and are reminded about what they have been praised for. Children enjoy praise and the stickers help them to replicate the good behaviour again.

Example stickers:

Think
Stickers may be personalised in a simple way just by writing on the child's name.

good lining up

good taking turns

good listening

Creating Practical Rewards

Resources needed

Large pieces of paper (A2 or A3 size)
Colouring pens, pencils, crayons or paints
Scissors

Activity and key ideas

Rewards can get to be monotonous for children. When too many stickers are given out they lose their meaning and are no longer exciting.

Try creating a reward system that can be built up over time. Ask the children to draw or paint a giant picture of a smiley face. Colour it in with a bright red smile and nice bright hair.

Cut the picture into six or eight segments. Each time the children in the setting do something that is worthy of praise, pin a segment of the picture up on the wall. When the whole picture is complete the group or class receive a special reward such as extra playtime or extra stories.

Think

For children who have a special interest or obsession, use a relevant picture, cut it up into pieces and each time the child needs praising paste a bit of the picture into a page of a private reward book. Once the picture is complete the child is given an egg timer and their special toy, and allowed time to play with their item of special interest.

Positive Praise Medals

Resources needed
Card
Scissors
Colouring pens, pencils, crayons or paints

Activity and key ideas
Engage the children in making their own reward medals. Cut out a simple self-standing medal shape. Fold along the dotted line so the medal stands up on a desk.

Draw a star or thumbs up onto the medal front and colour it in.

When the child deserves praise, reward their behaviour by giving them the medal to have on their table for the session.

Think
Raise self-esteem and confidence by writing on the medal *I did it!* The obvious question from other people is then to ask the child what they did, giving the child the chance to tell why they were awarded the medal and for positive praise to be reinforced.

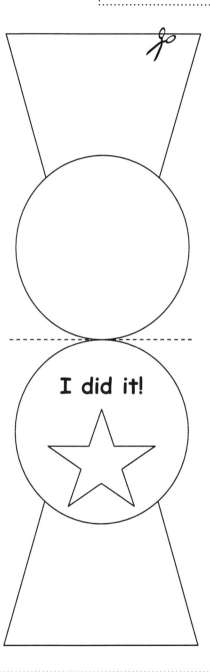

I did it!

Conclusion and Useful Resources

All the ideas in this book can be adapted to ensure they are appropriate and suitable for all children. Always consider the activities from the child's perspective and take a child-centred approach. The world is a very different place seen through the eyes of a child. Consider what you are saying and how you are saying it. Does it make sense to the child or is it confusing?

Consider your language and the child's own learning style. Try to make your behaviour responsive to the child's understanding. The more we know our children the better we will be able to respond effectively to promote positive behaviour.

Useful Resources

Talk about ... Emotions photographic cards published by Yellow Door
Emotion Stones: a set of 12 emotion faces on tactile pebbles, published by Yellow Door
www.yellow-door.net

Widgit symbols software www.widgit.com

For further information on the ideas in this book and to see other practical visual and kinaesthetic resources visit The Play Doctors: www.theplaydoctors.co.uk

Author Wendy Usher has worked with children and young people for over 30 years particularly those with special needs or disabilities. She is married with two grown up daughters, one of whom happens to be on the autism spectrum. She has three young granddaughters.

Wendy started up The Play Doctors in 2007 to design visual resources for children and is the author of several further books published by The Play Doctors.

Learning Style Observation Record

LEARNING STYLE OBSERVATION RECORD
(allowing free choice and control of play)

Name of child	Date
Primarily auditory activities	**Primarily kinaesthetic activities**
Primarily visual activities	**Notes of observation**

Record of any underlying impairments or known traits

Communication Assessment

COMMUNICATION ASSESSMENT

Name of child		Date	
What works well		**What does not work so well**	
Special ways in which the child communicates			

Communication Passport

All about me

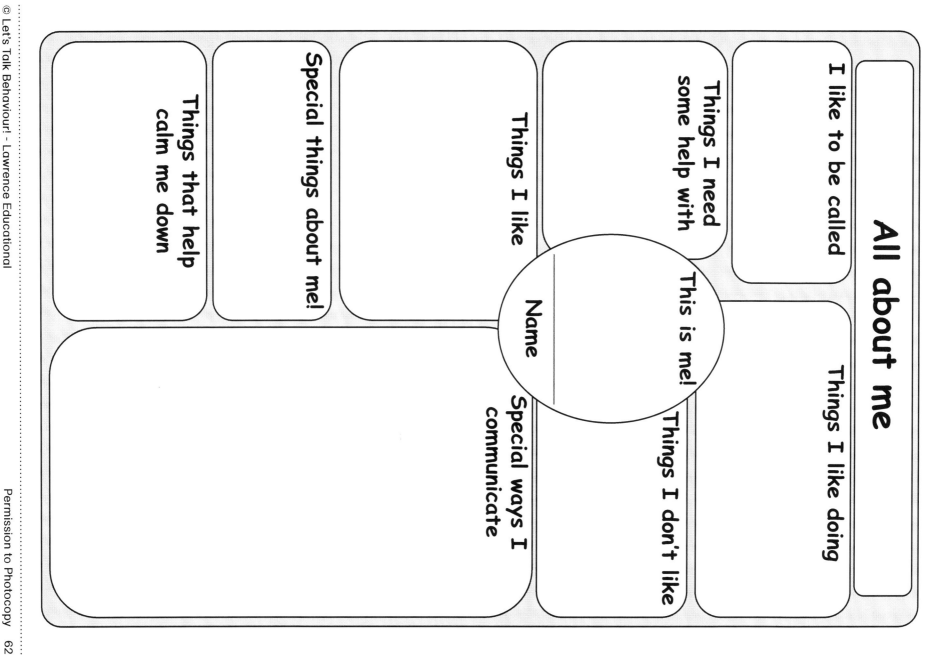

I like to be called

Things I need some help with

Things I like

Special things about me!

Things that help calm me down

This is me!

Name

Things I like doing

Things I don't like

Special ways I communicate